TRAVELLER
WITHOUT LUGGAGE

by the same author

RING ROUND THE MOON

ANTIGONE and EURYDICE

THIEVES' CARNIVAL

TIME REMEMBERED

THE LARK

RESTLESS HEART

DINNER WITH THE FAMILY

ARDÈLE and COLOMBE

TRAVELLER
WITHOUT LUGGAGE

by

JEAN ANOUILH

Translated by

JOHN WHITING

METHUEN & CO LTD
36 Essex Street London WC2

This play is fully protected by copyright. All inquiries concerning the rights of professional stage production should be addressed to Dr Jan van Loewen Ltd, International Copyright Agency, 81–83 Shaftesbury Avenue, London W1, and of amateur stage production to Samuel French Ltd, 26 Southampton Street, London WC2

This translation first published in 1959
© 1959 by Jean Anouilh and John Whiting
Printed in Great Britain
by W. & J. Mackay & Co Ltd, Chatham
Cat. No. 6258/U

This play was first presented in London at the Arts Theatre on 29th January 1959, with the following cast:

GASTON (*a man who has lost his memory*)	Denholm Elliott
GEORGES RENAUD (*his presumed brother*)	Geoffrey Keen
MADAME RENAUD (*the presumed mother of Gaston*)	Irene Brown
VALENTINE RENAUD (*wife to Georges*)	Elizabeth Sellars
THE DUCHESSE DUPONT-DUFORT (*a lady of charity*)	Joyce Carey
MAÎTRE HUSPAR (*a solicitor in Gaston's interests*)	Douglas Wilmer
A SMALL BOY	Hugh James
MR PICWICK (*the small boy's lawyer*)	Norman Pitt

A BUTLER		Anthony Blake
A CHAUFFEUR	*Servants*	James Wellman
A VALET	*of the*	John Warner
A COOK	*Renaud household*	Peggyann Clifford
JULIETTE		Violetta

The play directed by PETER HALL

Décor by TOM KEOGH

SCENE ONE

The drawing-room of a substantial country house, with a wide view over a formal garden. When the curtain rises the room is empty, then the DUCHESSE DUPONT-DUFORT, MAÎTRE HUSPAR *and* GASTON *are shown in by the* BUTLER.

BUTLER. What name shall I give, Madame?

DUCHESSE. The Duchesse Dupont-Dufort, Maître Huspar, the lawyer, and Monsieur – (*she hesitates*) – Monsieur Gaston. (*To* HUSPAR.) We shall have to call him that until further notice.

BUTLER (*who seems to understand the situation*). Please forgive Monsieur and Madame, but Madame la Duchesse was not expected until the eleven-fifty train. I will at once inform Monsieur and Madame that Madame la Duchesse is here.

DUCHESSE (*watching him go*). The butler is faultless. It makes me ridiculously happy, Gaston. I was sure you came of a good family.

HUSPAR. Don't be too optimistic. Remember, there are still five other families, beside these Renauds.

DUCHESSE. Yet something tells me that Gaston is going to recognize the Renauds as his, and that it's in this house he'll find his past. Something tells me that it's here he'll recover his memory. A woman's instinct, which rarely deceives.

HUSPAR (*bowing before such an argument*). Oh, well . . . In that case . . .

7

GASTON *is standing looking at the pictures in the room without much interest, like a bored child on a visit.*

DUCHESSE (*summoning him*). Well, Gaston, you are very moved, I trust.

GASTON. Not very.

DUCHESSE (*sighing*). Not very. I sometimes wonder, my dear boy, if you really understand how poignant your case is.

GASTON. But, Madame la Duchesse . . .

DUCHESSE. No, no! Nothing will make me say otherwise. You do not understand. Come now, confess it.

GASTON. Perhaps not very well, Madame la Duchesse.

DUCHESSE (*satisfied*). All the same, you're a charming boy, ready to admit your faults. I've always said that. But the fact remains that we cannot approve your very casual attitude. Isn't that so, Huspar?

HUSPAR. Good Lord, I . . .

DUCHESSE. No, I must make him understand that he should be moved by his situation.

GASTON *has returned to stare at the paintings.*

Gaston!

GASTON. Madame?

DUCHESSE. Are you made of stone?

GASTON. Stone?

DUCHESSE. Yes. Is your heart harder than rock?

GASTON. I – I don't think so, Madame.

DUCHESSE. Good answer. No more do I think so. But to someone knowing you less well than we do you would seem to be a man of marble.

GASTON. Really?

DUCHESSE. Gaston, perhaps you don't understand the seriousness of what I'm saying. I sometimes forget that

8

I'm speaking to a man who has lost his memory. There must be words that you have not heard for eighteen years. Do you know what to be like marble means?

GASTON. To be like stone.

DUCHESSE. Quite right. But, more important, what kind of stone? The hardest stone, Gaston. Do you understand?

GASTON. Yes.

DUCHESSE. Does it mean nothing to you that I compare your heart to the hardest stone?

GASTON (*at a loss*). Well – (*he pauses*) – well, more than anything, it rather tickles me.

DUCHESSE. D'you hear that, Huspar?

HUSPAR (*settling the business*). He's a child.

DUCHESSE (*peremptorily*). It's not childishness, it's ingratitude. (*To* GASTON.) You are one of psychiatry's most worrying cases, the most distressing riddle of the Great War, and that – if I understand your vulgar language – that makes you laugh. A talented journalist has very rightly called you the living unknown soldier, and you seem to find it comic. Are you quite incapable of respect, Gaston?

GASTON. But since I'm the person in question . . .

DUCHESSE. That has nothing to do with it! In the name of all you represent, you must forbid yourself to laugh at yourself. It may seem even funnier when I tell you in all sincerity that on seeing yourself in a looking-glass you should lift your hat to yourself.

GASTON. Should I? To myself?

DUCHESSE. To yourself! We all do it in thinking of what you represent. Who do you think you are that you should be exempt?

GASTON. No one, Madame.

DUCHESSE. Bad answer. You think yourself very important. The fuss the newspapers made about your case has gone to your head, that's what it is.

GASTON *tries to speak.*

Not a word! You'll displease me!

GASTON *lowers his eyes and goes back to the paintings.*

How do you find him, Huspar?

HUSPAR. Unconcerned, as usual.

DUCHESSE. Unconcerned. That's the word. It's been on my
mind for days, but I couldn't bring myself to say it.
Unconcerned! That's what he is. However, it's his own
fate the foolish boy is playing with. We've not lost our
memories, have we, Huspar: we're not searching for our
family?

HUSPAR. Certainly not.

DUCHESSE. No.

HUSPAR (*shrugging his shoulders: resigned*). To you, this is
a new cause. But don't forget, his lack of interest has
frustrated our efforts for years.

DUCHESSE. It's unforgivable that he doesn't acknowledge
the trouble my nephew has taken. You know he's cared
for Gaston with splendid devotion, all his heart in the
task! I hope he told you the result before you came
away.

HUSPAR. Doctor Jibelin wasn't at the asylum when I went
to get Gaston's documents. Unfortunately, I couldn't
wait for him.

DUCHESSE. Do you mean you didn't see darling Albert
before you left? Then you don't know the news.

HUSPAR. What news?

DUCHESSE. During the last blistering Albert succeeded in
making Gaston speak in his delirium. Oh, he didn't say
much. He said: "Little Pisser".

HUSPAR. Little Pisser?

DUCHESSE. Yes, Little Pisser. You may tell me that it's of

10

no importance, but what is so interesting is that it's a phrase which, normally, no one had ever heard him say, and no one remembered having said in front of him. Therefore, it's very likely to have come from his past.

HUSPAR. Little Pisser?

DUCHESSE. Little Pisser. A small clue, certainly, but it's something. His past is no longer an unlit cavern. Who knows? This Little Pisser may put us on the right road. (*She meditates.*) Little Pisser. The nickname of a friend, perhaps. A homely oath, for all I know. But at least we have a starting point now.

HUSPAR (*also in thought*). Little Pisser . . .

DUCHESSE (*repeating it, delighted*). Little Pisser. I shall never forget when Albert burst into the room to tell me his astonishing findings. "Aunt," he said, "my patient has spoken a word from his past: a swear word." I held my breath. I was afraid of an obscenity. The fact that so charming a boy might be of low birth appalled me. Was it that which kept Albert awake at night? The poor child was becoming so thin. Had he questioned Gaston and blistered his buttocks only to have him recover his memory and say that before the war he was a brick-layer! Something told me otherwise. I am a romantic, my dear Huspar. Something told me that my nephew's patient was a very celebrated man. I liked to think he was a playwright. A great playwright.

HUSPAR. It's hardly likely that he was a well-known man. He would already have been recognized.

DUCHESSE. The photographs were all bad. And war is an ordeal, you know.

HUSPAR. Anyway, I don't remember hearing of any well-known playwright reported missing during hostilities. That kind of person notifies the newspapers of his

11

smallest action, let alone his total disappearance.

DUCHESSE. Huspar, you're cruel! You're destroying a beautiful dream. All the same, he's a gentleman, I'm sure of that. See how attractive he is in those clothes. I had him dressed by Albert's tailor.

HUSPAR (*putting on his eyeglasses*). Well, do you know, I said to myself: surely that's not the asylum uniform . . .

DUCHESSE. I couldn't have him living at the château and visiting these families with me, dressed in grey flannelette.

HUSPAR. These confrontations in the home are an excellent idea.

DUCHESSE. Aren't they? That's what dear Albert told Gaston as soon as he took him in hand. What was needed to rediscover his past was to plunge him into the very atmosphere of that past. From that to taking Gaston round to the four or five families holding the most convincing proof was only a step. But Gaston was not Albert's only patient. It was out of the question for Albert to leave the asylum for the actual meetings. He might have asked the Ministry to organize a wholesale mustering, but you know how mean those people are. So what would you have done in my place? I answered: "I am here!" As in 1914.

HUSPAR. Fine example!

DUCHESSE. In Doctor Bonfant's time the families went willy-nilly to the asylum every Monday, saw Gaston for a few minutes, and returned by the first train. Who could find his mother and father in such conditions? Doctor Bonfant is dead. Very well. We must say nothing. But the least we could say, if the silence of the tomb was not sacred, is that Bonfant was a duffer and a blackguard.

HUSPAR. A blackguard, oh . . .

12

DUCHESSE. Don't try to keep me quiet! I wish he wasn't dead so that I could throw the word in his face. Blackguard! It's all his fault that this wretched man has dragged along in asylums since 1918. When I think that Bonfant kept him at Pont-au-Bronc for nearly fifteen years without making him speak a word of his past, whilst Albert, who has only had him three months, has already made him say "Little Pisser", I am dumbfounded. Albert is a great psychiatrist.

HUSPAR. And a charming young man.

DUCHESSE. A dear boy. With him, happily, everything is being changed. Meetings, examination of handwriting, police inquiries, nothing which is humanly possible is spared in order that his patient should find his real life again. As well as the usual clinical treatment, Albert decided to use the most modern methods. Think of it, he's already given Gaston seventeen blisterings.

HUSPAR. Seventeen? That's incredible!

DUCHESSE (*delighted*). Incredible. And very brave on Albert's part. He admitted it was risky.

HUSPAR. But what about Gaston?

DUCHESSE. What right had he to complain? It was all for his good. He had a backside like a colander, I've no doubt, but he found his past. And our past is the best of ourselves. What man of spirit would hesitate between his past and the skin of his bottom?

HUSPAR. The question does not usually arise.

DUCHESSE (*noticing* GASTON, *as he passes close to her*). You're very grateful to Doctor Jibelin, aren't you, Gaston – after the years lost by Doctor Bonfant – for his efforts in helping you to recover your memory?

GASTON. Very grateful, Madame.

DUCHESSE (*to* HUSPAR). I didn't make him say it. (*To* GASTON.) Ah! Gaston, isn't it affecting to think that

13

beyond that door beats a mother's heart, and there is an old father ready to hold out his arms to you?

GASTON (*like a child*). You know, I've had so many nice old women deceiving themselves and kissing me with wet noses, and mistaken old men scratching me with their beards. I am a man with nearly four hundred families, Madame. And every one of them is obstinately set on cherishing me. It's a lot.

DUCHESSE. But the little children, the bambinos! The bambinos who wait for their father. Do you dare to say that you don't long to take them in your arms, and bounce them on your knee?

GASTON. It wouldn't be very proper, Madame. The youngest would be about twenty.

DUCHESSE. Ah! Huspar, he feels he must profane the most sacred things.

GASTON (*suddenly thoughtful*). Children. Yes, I'd have had children now, if I'd been allowed to live.

DUCHESSE. You know very well it was impossible.

GASTON. Why? Because I could remember nothing before an evening in Spring 1918, when I was found in a railway siding.

HUSPAR. Exactly, alas.

GASTON. It frightened people, I suppose, that a man could live without a past. At first, foundlings are looked at askance. But there comes a time when a few little ideas can be put in their heads. But a grown man, with hardly a country, no native town, no traditions, no name. What a bloody scandal!

DUCHESSE. You also prove, Gaston, that you had no education. I've told you not to use that word.

GASTON. Scandal?

DUCHESSE. No. (*She hesitates.*) The other.

GASTON (*again in thought*). No police record, either. Have

14

you ever thought of that, Madame? You trust me with your silver at table, and my room at the château is only a step from yours. Suppose I once killed somebody?

DUCHESSE. Your eyes deny it.

GASTON. You're lucky to have their trust. Sometimes, for something better to do, I look into them myself, and try to see a little of what they have seen. I see nothing.

DUCHESSE (*smiling*). All the same, you've never killed a man. We don't have to know your past to know that.

GASTON. I was found beside a train which had brought prisoners from Germany. Obviously, I had been at the front. Like the rest, I must have used weapons. A man's body needs no more than a rose thorn to make it bleed. Oh! I know I'm clumsy, and in war it is more important to the officers to fire a lot of bullets than to be accurate. So, let's hope I didn't hit anyone.

DUCHESSE. Nonsense! I like to think that you were a hero. I was talking about men killed in peacetime.

GASTON. A hero? That's very uncertain in war. The miser, the sneak, even the coward are compelled by the regulations to be heroes together, and in very much the same way.

DUCHESSE. Don't worry. Something tells me that you were a very well brought up boy.

GASTON. That doesn't mean I haven't done anything wrong. I must have hunted animals. All well brought up boys hunt. Let's hope that everyone laughed at me as a hunter, and that I missed the animals too.

DUCHESSE. My dear boy, we're very kind to listen to all this without laughing at you. You're far too squeamish!

GASTON. I was so contented at the asylum. I was standing in for myself. I got to know myself very well, and then I had to leave to search for another person to put on, like an old coat. I've never drunk anything but water;

15

perhaps tomorrow I shall find I'm a lamplighter's son who needs four litres of red wine a day. I've never had much patience; perhaps I shall find I'm a draper's son, who must collect and classify thousands of buttons.

DUCHESSE. I chose to start with these Renauds because they are good class people.

GASTON. Which means they have a beautiful house, and a faultless butler. But what kind of son have they?

DUCHESSE (*seeing the* BUTLER *coming in*). We shall know in a moment.

She stops the BUTLER *with a gesture.*

Just a minute. Don't bring them in yet. Gaston, go into the garden for a while. We'll have you called.

GASTON. Very well, Madame la Duchesse.

DUCHESSE (*taking him aside*). One more thing. There is no need to call me Madame la Duchesse. It was proper when you were my nephew's patient.

GASTON. Very well, Madame.

DUCHESSE. And don't try looking at them through the keyhole.

GASTON (*going*). I'm in no hurry. I've already seen three hundred and eighty-seven.

DUCHESSE (*watching him go*). Sweet boy. I shudder when I think of Doctor Bonfant putting him to plant lettuces! (*To the* BUTLER.) You can bring them in now. (*She takes* HUSPAR'S *arm.*) I am deeply moved, my dear Huspar. I feel as if I am about to engage in a merciless struggle with fate, death, and all the obscure forces of the world. As you see, I am dressed in black. I felt it to be appropriate.

The RENAUDS *come in: provincial, upper-middle class.*

MME. RENAUD (*on the threshold*). What did I tell you? He's not here.

HUSPAR. We've asked him to stay in the garden for a few moments, Madame.

GEORGES. Let me introduce myself. I am Georges Renaud. (*Introducing the two women who are with him.*) My mother, and my wife.

HUSPAR. Lucien Huspar. I'm the lawyer looking after the sick man's affairs. Madame la Duchesse Dupont-Dufort, president of various charitable organizations at Pont-au-Bronc. In the absence of her nephew, Doctor Jibelin, who cannot leave the asylum, she has been good enough to take on the task of accompanying the invalid.

They, shake hands.

DUCHESSE. Yes, I am associated with my nephew's work in a small way. He has thrown himself into this case with such enthusiasm and faith . . .

MME. RENAUD. We're eternally grateful for the care he has given our little Jacques, Madame. It would have made me very happy to have told him so, could he have been here.

DUCHESSE. Thank you, Madame.

MME. RENAUD. Forgive me. Sit down. This is such a moving moment.

DUCHESSE. I understand so well, Madame.

MME. RENAUD. You must know how impatient we are. It's now two years since we went to the asylum for the first time.

GEORGES. And in spite of continual requests we've had to wait until today for a second interview.

HUSPAR. There are so many applications. Remember, there are four hundred thousand missing persons in France. Four hundred thousand families, very few of them prepared to give up hope, believe me.

MME. RENAUD. But two years, Monsieur! And you don't know the circumstances in which he was shown to us before. You are not to blame, Madame, neither is your nephew, for he was not the director of the asylum at that time. The patient was paraded before us in a crowd, so that we could not get near him. There were nearly forty of us, altogether.

DUCHESSE. The interviews arranged by Doctor Bonfant were an absolute scandal!

MME. RENAUD. Yes, they were a disgrace. But we were obstinate. My son was recalled on business, but my daughter-in-law and I stayed on in a hotel in the hope of arranging another meeting. We bribed one of the asylum attendants to get us an interview of several minutes, unhappily without result. Another time, my daughter-in-law took the place of a linen maid who was ill. She was with Jacques all one afternoon, but couldn't speak to him as they were never alone.

DUCHESSE (*to* VALENTINE). How romantic! Suppose someone had found out? I hope you know how to sew.

VALENTINE. Yes, Madame.

DUCHESSE. But you were never alone with him?

VALENTINE. No, Madame, never.

DUCHESSE. Ah, Bonfant! Bonfant, you were a rascal!

GEORGES. I can't understand how they could have hesitated between several families when we have given them ample proof.

HUSPAR. Yes, it's extraordinary. But, you know, even after our last cross-checking, which was very detailed, there still remain – besides you – five families with pretty well equal chances.

MME. RENAUD. Five, Monsieur! Impossible!

HUSPAR. Unfortunately not, Madame.

DUCHESSE (*reading from a list*). Brigaud, Bougran, Grigou,

18

Legropâtre and Madensale. Let me say that I began with you because you have all my sympathy.

MME. RENAUD. Thank you.

DUCHESSE. No, don't thank me. Those are my feelings. Your letter gave the impression of charming people, and it has been confirmed by this meeting. After you, God knows what sort of world we shall find ourselves in. There is a grocer, a gasman . . .

MME. RENAUD. A gasman?

DUCHESSE. Yes, Madame, a gasman. We live in an extraordinary age, when such people have pretensions. Don't be afraid. While I am alive no one shall give Gaston to a gasman.

HUSPAR. It was announced that these visits would be made in alphabetical order – which was the logical way of going about it – but as you would have been among the last, Madame la Duchesse Dupont-Dufort decided, perhaps a little unwisely, to take no notice and come to you first.

MME. RENAUD. Why do you say unwisely? Surely those in charge of the invalid are at liberty . . .

HUSPAR. Perhaps, Madame. But you must be aware of the emotional atmosphere – often self-interested, I'm afraid – which surrounds Gaston. His disability pension, which he's never been able to touch, puts a small fortune on his head. The interest and arrears make it more than two hundred and fifty thousand francs.

MME. RENAUD. What part can money play in such a tragic situation?

HUSPAR. A large part, unhappily, Madame. May I say a word about the patient's legal position?

MME. RENAUD. Later, Monsieur, if you please.

DUCHESSE. Maître Huspar has a statute book where others have a heart. But as he's very kind – (*she discreetly*

19

pinches HUSPAR) – he's going to find Gaston for us. At once.

HUSPAR (*giving up the struggle*). Very well, Mesdames. All I ask is that you don't throw yourselves at him, in tears, when you meet. Such things, repeated many times, upset him very much.

He goes out.

DUCHESSE. You must be impatient to see him again, Madame.

MME. RENAUD. Could a mother feel otherwise?

DUCHESSE. Ah! I am very moved. (*To* VALENTINE.) Did you know our patient? That is, the one you believe to be our patient.

VALENTINE. Yes, Madame. I told you. I was at the asylum.

DUCHESSE. Of course. How forgetful I am!

MME. RENAUD. My elder son, Georges, married Valentine very young. They were friends as children. You love each other very much, don't you, Georges?

GEORGES (*coldly*). Very much, Mother.

DUCHESSE. A brother's wife is almost a sister, isn't she?

VALENTINE (*humorously*). That's right, Madame.

DUCHESSE. You must be madly happy to see him again.

VALENTINE, *uneasy, looks at* GEORGES, *who answers for her.*

GEORGES. Very happy. As a sister would be.

DUCHESSE. I am a romantic! I dreamed – shall I tell you this? – I dreamed that a woman he loved passionately would be present to recognize him. And that they would kiss, for the first time since leaving that tomb of an asylum. I see it will not be like that.

GEORGES (*flatly*). No, Madame, it will not be like that.

DUCHESSE. So much for my beautiful dream!

She goes to the entrance.

Maître Huspar is a long time. Your park is so big, and he's so short-sighted. I'll wager he's lost.

VALENTINE (*quietly, to* GEORGES). Why are you looking at me like that? You're not going to drag up the past, are you?

GEORGES (*gravely*). When I forgave you it was forgotten.

VALENTINE. Then don't stare at me every time that old fool opens her mouth.

MME. RENAUD (*who has not heard, and very likely knows nothing of the incident to which they refer*). Dear, good Valentine. She's quite upset. Isn't it sweet of her to remember our little Jacques in that way, Georges?

GEORGES. Yes, Mother.

DUCHESSE. Ah! Here he is.

HUSPAR *comes in, alone.*

DUCHESSE. I was right! You haven't found him.

HUSPAR. Yes, I found him, but I didn't dare to disturb him.

DUCHESSE. What does that mean? What was he doing?

HUSPAR. He was standing in front of a statue.

VALENTINE (*crying out*). The Diana! The one with the curved bench at the end of the park.

HUSPAR. Yes. Look, you can see him from here.

Everyone looks.

GEORGES (*sharply*). Well, what does that prove?

DUCHESSE (*to* HUSPAR). This is exciting, my dear!

VALENTINE (*quietly*). I don't know. I seem to remember that he was very fond of that statue, and the bench.

DUCHESSE (*to* HUSPAR). We're getting warm, my dear, getting warm!

MME. RENAUD. You surprise me, Valentine. That corner of

21

the park was once part of Monsieur Dubanton's estate. We'd already bought it, certainly, in Jacques's time, but we didn't pull down the wall until after the war.

VALENTINE (*troubled*). I don't know, then. You must be right.

HUSPAR. His expression was so very strange as he stood in front of the statue, I didn't dare to disturb him before coming to ask you if it could be significant. As it isn't, I'll go and get him.

He goes out.

GEORGES (*quietly, to* VALENTINE). That bench was where you used to meet, was it?

VALENTINE. I don't know what you're talking about.

DUCHESSE. In spite of your understandable emotion, Madame, I beg you, be calm.

MME. RENAUD. You can trust me, Madame.

HUSPAR *comes in, with* GASTON.

(*She murmers*). It's Jacques. Yes, it's Jacques . . .

DUCHESSE (*going to* GASTON *and concealing him from the others with a tremendous theatrical gesture*). Gaston! Try to think of nothing! Go forward without seeing, without effort! Look deep into these faces . . .

Silence: all are still. GASTON *moves to* GEORGES, *looks at him, then at* MADAME RENAUD. *He stops for a moment in front of* VALENTINE. *She whispers imperceptibly.*

VALENTINE. Darling . . .

GASTON *looks at her, surprised. Then he goes on, returning to the* DUCHESSE. *He gently raises his arms in a gesture of helplessness.*

22

GASTON (*courteously*). I am so very sorry . . .

CURTAIN

SCENE TWO

*A Louis XV double door, closed, in front of which are gathered,
whispering, the Renauds' servants. The* COOK, *crouching
down, is looking through the keyhole. The others are
grouped around her.*

COOK (*to the other servants*). Wait, now wait. They're looking
at him as if he's some queer animal. Poor boy, where can
he look himself, he wants to know . . .

CHAUFFEUR. See, let's see . . .

COOK. Wait now, wait. He's got up suddenly and upset
his cup. Looks as if he's had enough of their questions.
There now, there. Monsieur Georges takes him, ah yes,
over to the window, yes, there by the arm, gently now,
as if all's right. All right, yes . . .

CHAUFFEUR. All right . . .

JULIETTE. If you'd heard him – Monsieur Georges, I mean –
heard him when he found their letters after the war.
Seemed as mild as milk he did but underneath things,
oho yes, yes, were beginning to buzz . . .

VALET. Let me tell you this then, let me tell you he was
right as a husband, right . . .

JULIETTE (*fiercely*). Right, was he? Was it right to insult a
dead man? You think then, do you, it's right to louse
the dead . . .

VALET. It's not the dead go to bed with our girls . . .

JULIETTE. You, since you got married, you've thought of
nothing else, nothing. No, it's not the dead go to bed
with your girls. They've no chance, poor things: it's the

23

living do it, for the dead men can't come into it, now can they . . .

VALET. Too easy that, I'd say. You hop into bed, jigajig, and out to die. All right to be dead then . . .

JULIETTE. All right to be dead, is it? Fine, fine all right . . .

VALET. But to be left with the girl, the girl who . . .

JULIETTE. You've got it on the brain, haven't you? You go on and on till you're back where you started . . .

COOK (*pushed by the* CHAUFFEUR). Wait, wait. Now they're all getting together and yes, they're showing him photographs . . . (*Giving up her place.*) You could see through old-fashioned keyholes but these modern things . . . well, simple: you don't bother to look.

CHAUFFEUR (*bending down in his turn*). That's him! It's him! Yes, I know the little bastard's pugmug . . .

JULIETTE. Now why say that, eh? Why not shut your own pugmug . . .

VALET. Stick up for him, you do, eh? Can't you do like us . . .

JULIETTE. I liked Monsieur Jacques very much, and how can you talk? Didn't know him, did you? But I, I liked him very much . . .

VALET. Was your boss, he was. Blacked his boots, you did . . .

JULIETTE. Why not, since I liked him, why not? Got nothing to do with it . . .

VALET. Like his brother, a proper cow . . .

CHAUFFEUR (*giving up his place to* JULIETTE). Bad to worse, I'd say. Yes, it's him. The one who used to keep me waiting outside some kip till four in the morning till I was frozen, till he came out loaded. The stink of drink from him coming first by ten feet, till he was in the car throwing up. Yes, spew all over the cushions, the little sod . . .

24

COOK. Say it again, yes again, for it was me had to mop it up again and again. And to think he was just eighteen, only eighteen . . .

CHAUFFEUR. Come Christmas, his tip was a dirty word . . .

COOK. Some got worse. Remember the little kitchen boy then, that time? Each time it was a kick for him . . .

CHAUFFEUR. And for no reason. No, a real little sod he was, and when I heard he'd joined the greater number in 1918, well, I was the same as everybody, no worse, in saying good, it's a good thing . . .

BUTLER. Now, now, we must all move now . . .

CHAUFFEUR. You don't see it our way then, Monsieur Jules?

BUTLER. I could say more about it than you, for I heard their scenes at table and I was there when he nearly struck Madame . . .

COOK. His mother! At eighteen, only eighteen . . .

BUTLER. And yes, I know all the stories about Madame Valentine in detail, yes . . .

CHAUFFEUR. Let me say this then, Monsieur Jules: that I think it's very good of you to have shut your eyes to it all . . .

BUTLER. The affairs of the master are the master's affairs . . .

CHAUFFEUR. Yes, but with such a little bastard . . . Move over and let me have another look at him . . .

JULIETTE (*giving up her place*). Yes, I'm sure it's Monsieur Jacques, sure. He was a nice boy then, you know. Good looking, gentlemanly . . .

VALET. Let it go now, will you? You know there are other nice boys, younger too . . .

JULIETTE. Yes, nearly twenty years. It is quite a time. I wonder if he'll find me changed much. I wonder . . .

VALET. Why should it matter to you?

JULIETTE. No reason, no, none . . .

25

VALET (*after some thought, as the other servants make faces behind his back*). Here, you now. You sort of sighed when you thought he might be back. Now, why . . .

JULIETTE. I did, did I? No reason, no, none . . .

The other servants giggle.

VALET. Why're you fussing about in the mirror, now why? Did you want to know if you'd changed?

JULIETTE. I did, did I?

VALET. How old were you when he went to the war?

JULIETTE. Fifteen . . .

VALET. And the postman was your first . . .

JULIETTE. The postman, I've already told you. Yes, the postman who gagged, bound, and drugged me . . .

The other servants snigger.

VALET. You're sure the postman was your first?

JULIETTE. What a question! It's one of the things a girl remembers. Yes, and how he couldn't find time to put down his bag, the animal, and his letters fell out all over the kitchen . . .

CHAUFFEUR (*still at the keyhole*). Valentine, that girl Valentine can't stop looking at him. Ah, if he stays, I bet old Georges will have to put his purse in his pocket . . .

BUTLER (*taking his place*). Disgusting!

CHAUFFEUR. Perhaps he likes them like that.

They laugh.

VALET. They make me laugh a lot with their "'mnesia". Now, you'd think that if—well, if that's his family, he'd have recognized them by now, since this morning. Ask me, "'mnesia's" got nothing to do with it . . .

COOK. Don't know, no. There're times when I can't remember if I've put salt in the sauce . . .

VALET. But a family . . .

COOK. He's looking for something else, not a family in there, the scamp, eh . . .

BUTLER (*at the keyhole*). No doubt about it, he's back. It's him, I bet my head . . .

COOK. All the same, you know, they say there's five more families with good proof, as good as . . .

CHAUFFEUR. Let me say this about it. Let me tell you now. We shouldn't, nobody shouldn't wish that that little sod shouldn't be dead, no . . .

COOK. Ah, no . . .

JULIETTE. Like to see you all dead, I would . . .

BUTLER. No, certainly we shouldn't want that even for him, no. For lives begun like that never end well, never . . .

CHAUFFEUR. But suppose he found life in the asylum quiet and easy: good, too. What's he got to learn? What about the Grandchamp kid, about Valentine, about the half-million trick and all the other things we don't know even . . .

BUTLER. Yes, I wouldn't want to be in his place. No, rather mine . . .

VALET (*who is looking through the keyhole*). Look out, they're getting up. Coming out by the hall door . . .

The servants scatter.

JULIETTE (*as she goes*). But Monsieur Jacques, you know . . .

VALET (*following her, suspicious*). What? What about him . . .

JULIETTE. Nothing . . .

They have gone.

CURTAIN

SCENE THREE

JACQUES RENAUD'S *room, and the long, dark corridors of the old house which lead to it. On one side there is a paved hall which ends in a wide stone staircase with wrought iron banisters.* MADAME RENAUD, GEORGES *and* GASTON *appear by the stairs, and cross the hall.*

MME. RENAUD. Excuse me, I'll go first. This is the way to your room.

She opens the door.

And this is your room.

All three come into the room.

How careless! I asked especially that they open the shutters.

She opens them. The room, filled with light, is shown to be in the exact style of 1910.

GASTON (*looking about him*). My room . . .
MME. RENAUD. You asked that it should be decorated according to your own ideas. You had very modern taste.
GASTON. I must have liked convolvuluses and buttercups more than anything.
GEORGES. Oh, you were very daring, even then.
GASTON. So I see.

He notices an absurd article of furniture.

What on earth is that? A storm-tossed tree?
GEORGES. No, it's a music stand.
GASTON. Was I fond of music?
MME. RENAUD. We wanted you to learn the violin, but you

28

wouldn't have it. You lost your temper when we tried to make you practise, and kicked the instrument to pieces. That music stand was the only thing to resist.

GASTON (*smiles*). It was wrong. (*He goes to a portrait.*) Is that your son?

MME. RENAUD. Yes, that's you. When you were twelve years old.

GASTON. I see myself as being fair and timid then.

GEORGES. Your hair was very dark chestnut. You played football all day, and you were always smashing things.

MME. RENAUD (*showing* GASTON *a large trunk*). Look! I had it brought down from the attic.

GASTON. What's that? My old trunk? You'll soon make me believe I lived back in the Restoration.

MME. RENAUD. No, you silly boy, it was Uncle Gustave's trunk. But these are your toys.

GASTON (*opening the trunk*). My toys! Did I have toys? Of course I must have had them. But I'd forgotten.

MME. RENAUD. Look. Your catapult.

GASTON. A catapult. That doesn't look like a toy, does it?

MME. RENAUD. You killed birds with it. You were a little terror. The birds in the garden were not enough for you. No. I had an aviary of prize birds. One day you went in and killed them all!

GASTON. Birds? Innocent birds?

MME. RENAUD. Yes.

GASTON. How old was I?

MME. RENAUD. Seven, perhaps nine . . .

GASTON (*shaking his head*). I didn't do that.

MME. RENAUD. Yes, you did.

GASTON. No. When I was seven years old I'd go into the garden with breadcrumbs, and call the sparrows to eat from my hand.

GEORGES. You wrung the necks of the poor little things.

MME. RENAUD. Remember the dog whose paw he crushed with a stone.

GEORGES. And the mouse he led about on the end of a thread.

MME. RENAUD. And the squirrels. And later the weasels and polecats. You killed them! All of them! You had the prettiest stuffed. There's a whole collection of them upstairs. I must have them brought down. (*She rummages in the trunk.*) Here are your knives. Your first rifle . . .

GASTON (*also searching*). Isn't there a Punch and Judy or a Noah's Ark?

MME. RENAUD. You only wanted scientific toys when you were very small. Here's your gyroscope, and the test-tubes for making gunpowder. This is your electro-magnet. Your retorts and your mechanical crane.

GEORGES. We wanted to make a brilliant engineer of you.

GASTON (*bursting into laughter*). Of me?

MME. RENAUD. But you were happiest with your geography books. You always came first in geography.

GEORGES. When you were ten you could recite your Departments backwards.

GASTON. Backwards? Well, I've certainly lost my memory, for in the asylum I tried to learn them all over again, and even the right way round. Let's forget this trunk. We'll learn nothing from it. I don't see myself at all like that as a child.

> *He shuts the trunk and wanders about the room, touching various things and sitting in the armchairs. Suddenly he asks:*

Did this little boy have a friend? Another boy he was always with, swapping problems and postage stamps?

MME. RENAUD (*at once*). Of course you had many companions. Both at school and at the Club.

30

GASTON. Yes. Not companions, though. A friend. You see, before asking you what women I had . . .

MME. RENAUD (*shocked*). Jacques! You were little more than a child when you went away.

GASTON (*smiling*). All the same, I shall ask about that. But, first of all, it seems more important to ask what friend I had.

MME. RENAUD. Well, you can see them in the photographs of the school groups. After that, there were the people you went out with in the evening . . .

GASTON. But who did I like to go with best of all? Who did I confide in?

MME. RENAUD. You didn't really prefer anyone.

> She has spoken quickly, after a furtive glance at GEORGES. GASTON looks at her.

GASTON. So your son had no friend. That's a pity. I mean it's a pity if we find that I'm your son. There must be nothing more comforting, when you've become a man, than to see your childhood mirrored in the eyes of a small boy of once upon a time. Yes, a pity. For I'd rather hoped that I'd regain my memory through this imagined friend. It would be a perfectly natural thing for one person to do for another.

GEORGES (*after hesitating*). A friend – well, yes, you did have a friend you loved very much. You were even friends with him until you were seventeen. We didn't speak about him because it's a very painful story . . .

GASTON. Is he dead?

GEORGES. No, no, he's not dead. But you parted. You quarrelled. Irrevocably.

GASTON. Irrevocably, at seventeen? (*A pause.*) Do you know why we quarrelled?

GEORGES. Vaguely . . .

31

GASTON. And neither your brother nor this boy tried to see
each other again?

MME. RENAUD. You forget, there was the war. Since then,
well – you quarrelled over a small thing. You even came
to blows, as boys of that age do. And then without mean-
ing it, I'm sure, you did something – outrageous. Un-
lucky, what's more. You pushed him from the top of
some stairs. In falling, he injured his spine. He had to be
kept in plaster for a long time, and since then he's been
crippled. Now you'll understand how difficult and painful it would have been for you to try to see him again.

GASTON (*after a pause*). Yes, I understand. Where did they
have this quarrel? At school? At his house?

MME. RENAUD (*quickly*). No, here. But we won't say any
more about it. It's better not to remind you of such
things, Jacques.

GASTON. If I'm to remember one thing I must remember it
all, you know that very well. The past won't give itself
up in fragments. Where is this stairway? I'd like to see it.

MME. RENAUD. It's the one leading to your room, Jacques.
But what good will it do?

GASTON (*to* GEORGES). Will you show me?

GEORGES. If you like. But I really don't see why you want
to look at the place again . . .

They have moved to the landing.

MME. RENAUD. Well, that's it.

GEORGES. Yes, that's it.

GASTON (*looks around him; leans over the banisters*). Where
did we fight?

GEORGES. We've never found out, exactly. It was a maid-
servant who told us about the incident.

GASTON. Well, it wasn't something that happened every

day, so I expect she told it in detail. Where did we fight? This landing is quite wide . . .

MME. RENAUD. You must have fought right on the edge. You may even not have pushed him. Perhaps he slipped. Who can tell?

GASTON (*going back to her*). In that case, why didn't I go to see him every day and keep him company in his room? Why didn't I give up all my half-holidays, so that he didn't feel the injustice too much?

GEORGES. You each had your own story of what happened. General ill-feeling was mixed up with it . . .

GASTON. A servant saw us, you say? Which one?

MME. RENAUD. Do you need to know that? Anyway, the girl is no longer with us.

GASTON. Surely some of the other staff you have were here at that time? I'll ask them.

MME. RENAUD. I hope you'll not give too much credit to kitchen gossip. Question servants, and they'll always tell a fine story. You know what such people are.

GASTON (*returning to* GEORGES). Monsieur, I think you understand. As yet, I've remembered nothing here. All you've told me about your brother's childhood seems quite remote from what I believe myself to be. For the first time – perhaps because I'm tired, or for some other reason, I don't know – I feel troubled having people talk to me of their child.

MME. RENAUD. Dearest Jacques, I understand . . .

GASTON. There's no need to become affectionate. No need to call me, rather prematurely, dearest Jacques. We are here to make an inquiry, like the police. We must be as precise and if possible as callous as policemen. I am trying to come to know someone who is a complete stranger to me, and who I shall have to accept in a little while, perhaps, as part of myself. This strange marriage to a ghost is painful enough without coming into conflict with you as well. I will examine all the proof you have. I will hear all you have to say. But most important of all, I feel I must know the truth about that quarrel. The truth, however cruel it may be.

MME. RENAUD (*she begins to speak, hesitantly*). Well, in the silly way of young people you hit each other. You know how sensitive . . .

GASTON (*stopping her*). No, not you. That servant is still here, isn't she? You lied to me just now.

GEORGES (*suddenly, after a pause*). Yes, she's still here.

GASTON. Please send for her, Monsieur. Why hesitate? You must know that I shall find her and question her sooner or later.

GEORGES. It's so stupid. So terribly stupid.

GASTON. I'm not here to learn something pleasant. And if this is the incident which will give me back my memory, then you have no right to conceal it from me.

GEORGES. As you wish. I'll call her. (*He rings.*)

MME. RENAUD. You're trembling, Jacques. Are you ill?

GASTON. Trembling? Am I?

MME. RENAUD. Has something suddenly become clear to you?

GASTON. No. Nothing. Night. Darkest night.

MME. RENAUD. Then why are you trembling?

GASTON. It's silly. But of all possible memories it was the memory of a friend I needed most. I have built everything on this imaginary boy. Our solemn walks together, the books we discovered at the same time, a girl we were in love with at the same time. I gave her up. To him. I even – this will make you laugh – I even saved his life one day when we were boating. So, you see, if I am your son I must get used to things very different from my dreams.

JULIETTE *comes in.*

34

JULIETTE. Madame rang?

MME. RENAUD. Monsieur Jacques would like to speak to you, Juliette.

JULIETTE. To me?

GEORGES. Yes. He wants to ask you about the accident to Marcel Grandchamp, which you saw happen.

MME. RENAUD. You know the truth, girl. You know that even if Monsieur Jacques was violent, he never had a criminal thought.

GASTON (*interrupting her again*). Please don't say anything to her! Where were you, Mademoiselle, when the accident happened?

JULIETTE. On the stairs with the two gentlemen, Monsieur Jacques.

GASTON. Don't call me Monsieur Jacques. How did the quarrel start?

JULIETTE (*with a glance at the* RENAUDS). Well, you see . . .

GASTON (*turning to them*). Would you be so good as to leave me alone with her? I think you embarrass her.

MME. RENAUD. I'll do anything you wish, Jacques, if only you'll come back to us.

GASTON (*going with them to the door*). I'll call you. (*To* JULIETTE, *when they are alone.*) Sit down.

JULIETTE. May I, sir?

GASTON (*sitting opposite her*). Forget the formalities. They only get in the way. How old are you?

JULIETTE. Thirty-three. And you know it, Monsieur Jacques, because I was fifteen when you went to the front. Why ask me?

GASTON. Because I didn't know. Once again, I may not be Monsieur Jacques.

JULIETTE. Oh, yes, you are. I recognize you.

GASTON. Did you know him well?

35

JULIETTE (*suddenly in tears*). You never forget that sort of thing! Don't you remember anything at all, Monsieur Jacques?

GASTON. Absolutely nothing.

JULIETTE (*bawling through her tears*). To be asked such things after what happened! Oh, it can be torture to a woman.

GASTON (*pauses for a moment, confused; then suddenly, he understands*). Ah! Oh, forgive me. Please forgive me. So Monsieur Jacques . . .

JULIETTE (*snivelling*). Yes.

GASTON. Then I beg your pardon. How old were you?

JULIETTE. Fifteen. He was my first.

GASTON (*suddenly at ease, smiling*). Fifteen, and he was seventeen. That's a very sweet story. It's the first thing I've heard about him that seems at all sympathetic. Did it last long?

JULIETTE. Until he left.

GASTON. I have tried very hard to discover what my best friend looked like. Well, I find she was charming.

JULIETTE. Charming, maybe, but she wasn't the only one, you know.

GASTON (*smiling again*). No?

JULIETTE. No.

GASTON. Well, that's not so unsympathetic.

JULIETTE. Perhaps you find it funny. But you must admit that for a woman . . .

GASTON. Yes, certainly, for a woman . . .

JULIETTE. It's hard to feel herself laughed at in her tragic love affair.

GASTON (*a little bewildered*). In her tra. . . Yes, of course.

JULIETTE. I know I was only a little skivvy, but that didn't stop me from draining to the dregs the dreadful sorrow of an outraged lover.

36

GASTON. Dreadful . . .? Certainly not.

JULIETTE. Have you ever read *Raped on her Wedding Night*?

GASTON. No.

JULIETTE. You should. There's a very similar situation in it. Bertrande's infamous seducer has also left her. (But he went to America, whence he was summoned by his inordinately rich uncle.) And she says to him, Bertrande does, "I have drained to the dregs the dreadful sorrow of an outraged lover".

GASTON (*who is suddenly enlightened*). Oh, I see! It's a sentence from a book.

JULIETTE. Yes, but it applied very well to me.

GASTON. Quite.

He suddenly gets up. He asks, lightly:

Did Monsieur Jacques love you very much?

JULIETTE. Passionately. He said he would kill himself for me.

GASTON. How did you become lovers?

JULIETTE. It was the second day I was here. I'd just finished doing this room. Monsieur Jacques tumbled me on the bed. I laughed like an idiot. Using force at that age! Mind you, it all happened, as you might say, in spite of myself. But afterwards he swore that he'd love me for the rest of his life.

GASTON (*looks at her, and smiles*). Funny, coming from Monsieur Jacques . . .

JULIETTE. Why funny?

GASTON. Never mind. Anyway, if I do turn out to be Monsieur Jacques, I promise I'll talk to you about it all very seriously.

JULIETTE. Oh, I don't want amends. I've married since then.

GASTON. All the same . . . (*A pause.*) But I'm playing truant. I shall never pass my examination. Let's get back to

37

work, back to this wretched story we'd both like to forget, but which I have to know from beginning to end.

JULIETTE. You mean the fight with Monsieur Marcel?

GASTON. Yes. Were you there?

JULIETTE (*proudly*). Of course I was there.

GASTON. You were in at the beginning of their quarrel?

JULIETTE. Certainly I was.

GASTON. Then you'll be able to tell me what madness made them fight so savagely?

JULIETTE (*placidly*). What do you mean, madness? They were fighting for me.

GASTON (*rises*). For you?

JULIETTE. Of course. Are you surprised?

GASTON (*repeats, stunned*). For you?

JULIETTE. Yes! I was Monsieur Jacques's mistress. I've told you that because you wanted to know it, but no putting it around, eh? I don't want to lose my place for something that happened twenty years ago. Yes, I was Monsieur Jacques's mistress and, I'm afraid I'm going to have to tell you, Monsieur Marcel tried to trip me.

GASTON. Well?

JULIETTE. One day he tried to kiss me behind the door. I didn't let myself do it, see? But you know what a boy's like when he's got that in his head. Just then Monsieur Jacques came out of his room and saw us. He jumped at Monsieur Marcel, who dodged. Next thing, they were fighting, rolling on the ground . . .

GASTON. Where did they finish up?

JULIETTE. At the edge of the big first floor landing.

GASTON (*suddenly crying out, like a madman*). Where? Where? Where? Come, I want to see the exact place.

He has dragged JULIETTE *by the wrist to the landing.*

JULIETTE. You're hurting me!

GASTON. Where was it? Where?

JULIETTE (*breaking from him, rubbing her wrist*). All right, then. There! They fell there, half in the hall, half on the landing. Monsieur Marcel was underneath.

GASTON. But they were a long way from the edge, there! How could he have fallen down the stairs? Did they roll as they fought?

JULIETTE. No. Monsieur Jacques managed to be the first up, and he dragged Monsieur Marcel by the leg to the top of the stairs . . .

GASTON. And then?

JULIETTE. Then he pushed him, shouting: "You little swine, that'll teach you to mess about with other peoples' tarts!"

Silence.

He was a one, was Monsieur Jacques.

GASTON (*whispering*). And this was his friend!

JULIETTE. Yes, since they were six, and first went to school together.

GASTON. Since they were six.

JULIETTE. Oh, it's awful, I know. But there you are: love is stronger than all.

GASTON (*looking at her, and murmuring*). Love, yes, love. Thank you, Mademoiselle.

GEORGES *knocks at the door. Then, not seeing them in the room, goes to the hall.*

GEORGES. I'm taking it on myself to come back. You haven't called us, but Mamma's worried. Have you learnt what you wanted to know?

GASTON. Yes, thank you. I've learnt what I wanted to know.

JULIETTE *has gone.*

39

GEORGES. It's not a pleasant story, certainly. But I like to believe, in spite of everything, that it was an accident, nothing but childishness – you were only seventeen, remember – devilish childishness.

Silence: he is embarrassed.

What did she tell you?

GASTON. What she saw, I suppose.

GEORGES. Did she say you fought because you were rivals at the Club? Marcel had resigned for some personal reason. You were one of the opposing gang, and it's true, isn't it, that with your enthusiasm for sport . . .

GASTON *says nothing.* GEORGES *goes on.*

Anyway, that's the version I like to believe. The Grandchamps put about another story, which I've always refused to accept. Don't try to find out what it was. A beastly, wicked story.

GASTON (*looking at* GEORGES). Did you love him very much?

GEORGES. He was my brother, in spite of all he did. Because there were many other things. Ah! You were terrible.

GASTON. Whilst I still have the right, I insist that you say: he was terrible.

GEORGES (*with a sad smile at his memories*). Yes, terrible. You caused us so much worry. If you come back to us you'll have to learn of other things, even more serious than the fight. In that, at least, you have the benefit of the doubt.

GASTON. Is there more to know?

GEORGES. You were a child. Left to his own devices in a world in chaos. Mamma, with her rigid principles, clashed with you in a clumsy way. Her kindest word only increased the gulf between you. I'd not enough authority. You did something at first sight just silly, but it cost us

40

very dear. We older men were at the front. The young people of your age thought anything was allowed them. You decided to set about some mischief. Did you look upon it as just mischief? Or was that a pretext for getting what you wanted? You're the only person who can tell us that, if you recover your memory. You managed to bewitch – bewitch, yes, that's the word – an old friend of the family. You persuaded her to give you a large sum of money, nearly half a million francs. You made yourself out to be a kind of go-between. You had writing paper printed with the forged heading of a company – and you signed false receipts. One day, everything was discovered. But it was too late. Only a few thousand francs were left. You'd spent the rest in God knows what gambling houses and clubs with women and friends. Naturally, we had to pay it back.

GASTON. The happiness you feel about the possible return of your brother does you credit.

GEORGES (*looking away*). More than you think, Jacques.

GASTON. What? Is there something else?

GEORGES. We'll speak of that another time.

GASTON. Why another time?

GEORGES. It's better so. I'm going to call Mamma. She must be worried.

GASTON (*stopping him*). You can speak to me. I'm almost sure that I'm not your brother.

> GEORGES *looks at him in silence for a moment, and then says in a flat voice:*

GEORGES. All the same, you're very like him. You have his face. Yes, his face, but as if clouded by a storm.

GASTON (*smiling*). It's eighteen years! I expect your face has changed in that time, for I've not the pleasure of knowing it unlined.

GEORGES. Your face shows more than lines. It shows the passage of time. But in passing it has not hollowed out and hardened. No, it has sweetened and smoothed away. Yes, it is as if a storm of goodness had swept over your face.

GASTON. It's as well, for it seems your brother's face was not distinguished by kindness.

GEORGES. You're wrong. He was hard, certainly, and wanton. But – oh, I loved him very much, with all his faults. He was better looking than I am. Not more intelligent, I don't think – the kind of intelligence he needed at school – but he was more acute, more glittering, more – (*flatly*) – more seductive. He loved me, you know, in his way. When he began to grow up he had a sort of understanding tenderness towards me which touched me very much. That's why I was so hurt when I heard of it.

He lowers his head as if it were he who had been in the wrong.

I hated it all. Yes, hated it. Then, quite soon, I no longer knew what to feel.

GASTON. About what?

GEORGES (*looks up at* GASTON). Is that you, Jacques?

GASTON *makes a movement.*

I've often said to myself: he was young, he was weak at heart like all violent people. I've often said: everyone yields to beautiful lips on a summer night when they are going to war. And she, too, was very young . . .

GASTON. I don't follow you very well. Did he take something from you? A woman? Your wife?

GEORGES *indicates yes.*

42

(*Flatly*). The bastard.

GEORGES (*with a small, sad smile*). Perhaps it was you.

GASTON (*after a pause*). Your name's Georges, isn't it?

GEORGES. Yes.

> GASTON *looks at him for a moment, and then makes
> a clumsy gesture of tenderness.*

GASTON. Georges . . .

MME. RENAUD (*appearing in the ante-chamber*). Are you
there, Jacques?

GEORGES (*with tears in his eyes, ashamed of his emotion*).
Forgive me. I'll go. (*He goes out quickly, by the other door.*)

MME RENAUD (*coming into the room*). Jacques . . .

GASTON (*without moving*). Yes.

MME. RENAUD. Guess who's coming? It's an outrage!

GASTON (*wearily*). I have no memory. Now – riddles.

MME. RENAUD. Aunt Louise, my dear. Yes, Aunt Louise!

GASTON. Aunt Louise. And why is it an outrage?

MME. RENAUD. Well, it is after what happened. If you want
to please me you'll refuse to see her should she approach
you in spite of us. She behaves like that! You never liked
her. But the member of the family you really dislike –
hate, I think – and I must admit you once had cause, is
your cousin, Jules.

GASTON (*still without moving*). Then I hate someone without
knowing it.

MME. RENAUD. You don't know what the little wretch did
to you. He sneaked at the general examination because
you had a logarithm table. I have to tell you these things
so that you can put a good face on it with such people.
For example, there's Gerard Dubuc, who will come and
be as sweet as honey. Well, he got himself into the
Filière Company by slandering you to the board of
directors. And you had a much better chance because of

your uncle. I hope you'll slam the door in his face, and on all the others who played you false.

GASTON. A past is full of such pleasant things . . .

MME. RENAUD. On the other hand, there's dear Madame Bouquon. She was always a little repellant to you, because she's paralysed, poor thing. But you should give her a kiss. She saw you born.

GASTON. That doesn't seem to me sufficient reason.

MME. RENAUD. And she looked after you when you had pneumonia, and I was ill at the same time. She saved your life, dear.

GASTON. Of course. There's also gratitude. I'd forgotten that. (*A pause.*) Obligations, hatred, offences. Did I think only those were to be remembered? (*He stops, reflectively.*) It's true I've forgotten remorse. Now I have a complete past. (*He smiles, amused, and goes to* MADAME RENAUD.) But, you know, I'm hard to please. I'd have preferred the pattern to have some happiness. A little enthusiasm, too, if possible.

MME. RENAUD. I don't understand, dear.

GASTON. It's very simple. I'd like you to tell me one of my old pleasures. My hate and remorse have taught me nothing. So tell me of something that made your son happy, to see if that sounds like me.

MME. RENAUD. Oh, that's easy. Many things made you happy. You were so spoilt.

GASTON. Well, tell me one.

MME. RENAUD. All right. It's so confusing having to recall one like this, on the spur of the moment. I don't know which to choose . . .

GASTON. Give me one at random.

MME. RENAUD. Well – well, when you were twelve . . .

GASTON (*stopping her*). No. An adult pleasure. The others are too far off.

44

MME. RENAUD (*suddenly embarrassed*). It's just that – your grown up pleasures – well, you didn't tell me much about them. You were a gay boy, you went out a lot. Like all boys of that age you thought you were a king. You found your happiness with your friends. But with me . . .

GASTON. Did you never see me happy?

MME. RENAUD. Of course I did! Why, on your last prize day I remember . . .

GASTON (*interrupting*). No, not a prize day. Later. Between the day I finished with my school books and the day they put a gun in my hand. During those few months which turned out to be my whole adult life.

MME. RENAUD. I'm trying to think. You went out so much. You were such a man.

GASTON. However much we may play at being men when we're eighteen, we're still children. Surely, one day, there was a leak in the bathroom which no one could stop; or a day when the cook's mispronunciation was at its worst; or we came across a comic tram-conductor, and I laughed in front of you. Perhaps I was pleased with a present or a ray of sunshine. I'm not asking for something out of the ordinary. Just a small moment of happiness. Surely I wasn't quite morbid.

MME. RENAUD (*hesitating*). Very well, I'll tell you, Jacques. I'd rather have explained this later, and more calmly. At that time you and I were not on very good terms. Oh, it was childish! Looking back on it now, I'm sure it will seem to you much more serious than it was. But it's true: at that time, between leaving school and joining your regiment, we did not speak to each other.

GASTON. Ah!

MME. RENAUD. Yes. Oh, just stupidity, you know.

GASTON. And – did this quarrel last a long time?

MME. RENAUD. Nearly a year.

GASTON. Christ! We could certainly keep it up. Who began it?

MME. RENAUD (*after hesitation*). Oh, I did, if you like. But it was your fault really. You were very stubborn.

GASTON. What could make a young man so stubborn that you could not bring yourself to speak to him – your son – for a year?

MME. RENAUD. You did nothing to put an end to the business. Nothing!

GASTON. Had we made it up by the time I left for the front? Did you let me go without kissing me good-bye?

MME. RENAUD (*suddenly, after a silence*). Yes. (*A pause, then quickly.*) That day was your fault, too. I waited for you in my room. You stayed in yours. You wanted me, your mother, to make the first move, although you had hurt me so deeply. The others had tried to reconcile us. Nothing would make you give in. Nothing. So you left for the front.

GASTON. How old was I?

MME. RENAUD. Eighteen.

GASTON. Perhaps I didn't know what I was going to. War seems an amusing game at that age. But then, it wasn't 1914, when mothers put flowers on the guns. You must have known. You must have known what I was going to.

MME. RENAUD. I thought the war would be over before you left the barracks, or that I'd see you on leave before you went to the front. Anyway, you were always so abrupt and hard with me.

GASTON. But couldn't you have brought yourself to say: "You're mad. Kiss me!"

MME. RENAUD. I was afraid of the look in your eyes, and the arrogant grin I knew you'd have on your face. You were capable of hunting me down . . .

GASTON. Even so, you should have come and cried at my door, begging me on your knees not to do such a thing,

46

and that I should kiss you before going. It was wrong
not to do that!

MME. RENAUD. But I was your mother, Jacques . . .

GASTON. I was eighteen, and I was being sent to die. I am
a little ashamed to say this, but however brutal I'd been,
shut up in my crazy young pride, all of you should have
gone down on your knees and asked my forgiveness.

MME. RENAUD. Forgiveness! I'd done nothing!

GASTON. And what had I done to cause this breach between
us?

MME. RENAUD (*suddenly speaking as in the past*). You took
it into your head to marry a little dressmaker that you
picked up God knows where, and who, I suppose, refused to sleep with you. Marriage is not a love affair!
How could we let you compromise yourself and bring
that girl into the house? Don't tell me you loved her!
How can anyone be in love, deeply, lastingly in love at
eighteen? Enough in love to marry and set up house with
a little dressmaker's apprentice picked up at a dance
three weeks before.

Silence.

GASTON. Yes, of course it was foolish. But my class was
going to be called up in a few months. You knew that.
That affair might have been the only indiscretion I'd
have a chance to commit: the boy who begged you to
allow it had only a few months to live, hardly long enough
to be married.

MME. RENAUD. But we didn't think you were going to be
killed! Anyway, I've not told you everything. Do you
know what you shouted at me, with your mouth twisted
and your hand raised to strike? You shouted: "I hate
you! I hate you!" That's what you said to me, your
mother.

47

Silence. She goes on.

Now do you understand why I stayed in my room hoping that you would come up? Why I stayed there until the street door slammed behind you.

GASTON (*quietly, after a pause*). So I died at eighteen, never having had the smallest happiness because it might have been considered a foolishness, and with you never having spoken to me again. I lay on my back all one night with a wounded shoulder and I was twice as lonely as the others who called for their mother.

Silence. He says suddenly, as if to himself:

It's true. I hate you.

MME. RENAUD (*cries out, frightened*). Jacques, what's the matter?

GASTON (*coming back to himself, seeing her*). What? Sorry. I'm sorry. (*He is distant, shut away, inflexible.*) I am not Jacques Renaud. I remember nothing that was his in this place. There was a moment, certainly, hearing you speak, when I mistook myself for him. I'm sorry. A complete past is too much for any man to take on himself all at once. If you want to please me, more than that, be kind to me, you'll let me go back to the asylum. I planted lettuces and polished floors. The days passed, but even after eighteen years there – exactly one half of my life – the days never formed themselves into this ravening thing you call a past.

MME. RENAUD. But, Jacques . . .

GASTON. So don't call me Jacques any more. He's done too much, this Jacques of yours. Let it be Gaston; although he's a nobody, I know what he is. But Jacques, his name buried beneath the bodies of so many dead birds, who smiled, murdered, and went off to fight with no one to see him go, never in love, he frightens me.

48

MME. RENAUD. But in the end, my dearest . . .

GASTON. Go away! I'm not your dearest.

MME. RENAUD. You're speaking to me now as you did before!

GASTON. I have nothing to do with that earlier time. I am speaking to you now. Today. Go away!

MME. RENAUD (*straightens herself again: she too speaks as in the earlier days*). Very well, Jacques! I'll go. But when others have proved that I am your mother I shall expect you to come and ask forgiveness.

She goes out, not seeing VALENTINE, *who has heard the last words between them from the corridor.*

VALENTINE (*comes in when* MADAME RENAUD *has gone*). You said that he'd never been in love. How can you know that, if you know nothing?

GASTON (*staring at her*). You, too. Go away!

VALENTINE. Why speak to me like that? What's the matter?

GASTON (*shouting*). Go away! I am not Jacques Renaud!

VALENTINE. You shout as if you're scared.

GASTON. I am a little.

VALENTINE. It's understandable. Jacques's personality as a boy is quite something to take on. But why hate me?

GASTON. I don't like the way you smile. You've never stopped since I came here. You were his mistress.

VALENTINE. Who dared to say that?

GASTON. Your husband.

Silence.

VALENTINE. All right. What if you were my lover, and I want you back? Are you silly enough to think that wrong?

GASTON. You're speaking to a kind of primitive man. A bumpkin from a distant river with black waters and nameless shores. A man of so many years, but one come newly born into the world. So perhaps it's not so wrong, after all, to take a wife from a brother. A brother who loves and cares for her.

VALENTINE (*quietly*). When we knew each other during the holidays at Dinard I played tennis and swam with you more often than with your brother. The walks along the rocks were usually with you. It was you, and only you, I kissed. Later, when I came to your mother's parties, your brother fell in love with me. But it was you I came to see.

GASTON. All the same, it was he that you married.

VALENTINE. You were a baby. I was an orphan, penniless, under age, looked after by an aunt. She'd already taken it out of me for my other refusals of marriage. If I had to sell myself, surely it was better that it should be to the one man who would bring me nearer to you. Who else?

GASTON. There's usually a page in women's magazines which answers questions like that.

VALENTINE. I became your mistress on the return from the honeymoon.

GASTON. At least we waited a little while.

VALENTINE. A little while? Two awful months. But then we had three years all to ourselves, for the war broke out, and Georges left on August the fourth. Now, Jacques, after eighteen years . . .

She has put her hand on his arm. He draws away.

GASTON. I am not Jacques Renaud.

VALENTINE. That's as it may be. Let me look at the ghost of the only man I've ever loved. (*She smiles a little.*) Oh! you're screwing up your mouth. (*She is looking directly into his face: he is embarrassed.*) Does nothing about me –

50

a look, a way of speaking – match up with your few experiences?

GASTON. Nothing.

VALENTINE. Don't be so distant. It's a serious matter, you know, for a woman once in love to find after a long time, if not her lover, at least, from a slight twist of the mouth, her lover's ghost. His exact double.

GASTON. I may be an exact double: I am not Jacques Renaud.

VALENTINE. Look at me.

GASTON. I am looking at you. You're charming, but I'm not Jacques Renaud!

VALENTINE. Are you quite sure I mean nothing to you?

GASTON. Nothing.

VALENTINE. Well, then, you'll never recover your memory.

GASTON. I'm beginning to hope not. (*A pause. He is suddenly disturbed.*) Why did you say that?

VALENTINE. You don't even remember someone you saw two years ago.

GASTON. Two years ago?

VALENTINE. A linen maid. A temporary help.

GASTON. A linen maid? (*Silence. Suddenly he asks*) Who told you about that?

VALENTINE. No one. I took the part myself – with my mother-in-law's approval, what's more – so that I could get near you. Now look at me, man without a memory.

GASTON (*attracted by her in spite of himself: troubled*). Were you the linen maid who stayed one day?

VALENTINE. Yes.

GASTON. Why didn't you say something then?

VALENTINE. I didn't want to say anything before – I hoped, I believed, that by having me again you'd get back your memory.

GASTON. You said nothing afterwards.

51

VALENTINE. I nearly spoke then, but we were surprised. Remember?

GASTON (*smiling at the memory*). Of course. The matron.

VALENTINE (*also smiling*). Yes, the matron.

GASTON. But why didn't you shout aloud that you'd recognized me?

VALENTINE. I did. So did fifteen other families.

GASTON (*with a sudden nervous laugh*). Of course, I'm a fool! Everybody recognized me! So it doesn't prove that I'm Jacques Renaud.

VALENTINE. All the same, you remember the linen girl with the big bundle of sheets, don't you?

GASTON. Yes, I remember her. Apart from my amnesia, I've a good memory.

VALENTINE. Don't you want to make love to her again?

GASTON (*pushing her away*). We'll wait and see if I'm Jacques Renaud.

VALENTINE. And if you are?

GASTON. If I am I wouldn't make love to you again for anything in the world. I have no wish to be the lover of my brother's wife.

VALENTINE. You already have been!

GASTON. A long time ago. My misery since then has cleansed me of my youth.

VALENTINE (*with a triumphant little laugh*). You've already forgotten the linen maid! If you're Jacques Renaud you made love to your brother's wife just two years ago. You! Not some young boy away in the past.

GASTON. I am not Jacques Renaud.

VALENTINE. Listen to me, Jacques. You're going to have to give up the wonderful simplicity of life as a man without a memory. Listen, Jacques. You must accept yourself. Life, with it's fine morality and precious freedom, comes in the end to one thing: that we accept ourselves as we

52

are. The eighteen years in the asylum, keeping yourself pure and untouched, is the exact span of an adolescence. Your second adolescence, which ends today. You're going to become a man again. A man with all that that carries of sin, forgetfulness and happiness. Accept yourself, Jacques, and accept me.

GASTON. I may have to accept myself. I will never accept you.

VALENTINE. You've done so. Two years ago.

GASTON. I will not have my brother's wife!

VALENTINE. Forget the fine words. You'll find, now you're a man again, that none of your problems can be solved by a formula. You took me as that kind of man, yes. But the first Jacques had me as you are now. Simply because he'd become a man, master of his actions.

GASTON. There's not only you. I refuse to accept that I robbed old women, or raped servant girls.

VALENTINE. What servant girls?

GASTON. Another small point. I also refuse to accept that I nearly hit my mother, or any of this mad behaviour of my disgusting little double.

VALENTINE. Don't shout. But you did something of the kind just now . . .

GASTON. I told an inhuman old woman that I hate her. She is not my mother.

VALENTINE. Yes, Jacques, she is! And it's for that very reason that you spoke with such violence. You need only to be with the people from your past for a short time to take up your old attitude to them without thinking about it. Listen, Jacques. I'm going up to my room because you're going to lose your temper. You'll call me in ten minutes. For although you've a terrible temper, it never lasts longer than that.

GASTON. How do you know! You irritate me. You talk as if you know me better than I do myself.

VALENTINE. I do. Listen, Jacques. There is absolute proof, which I've never been able to tell the others . . .

GASTON (*drawing away from her*). I don't believe it!

VALENTINE (*smiling*). I haven't told you yet.

GASTON (*shouting*). I don't want to believe you! I don't want to believe anyone! All I want is that no one should speak of my past ever again!

The DUCHESSE *comes in, a whirlwind. She is followed by* MAÎTRE HUSPAR. VALENTINE *hides in the bathroom.*

DUCHESSE. Gaston! Gaston, this is frightful! Some people have arrived. They're furious, absolutely raving. It's one of your families. I had to receive them. They insulted me. I see now how foolish I was not to keep to the alphabetical order we announced in the papers. These people think they've been thwarted. They mean to create a scandal, and accuse us of God knows what!

HUSPAR. I'm sure, Madame, no one would dare to suspect you.

DUCHESSE. Don't you understand how blinded they are by these two hundred and fifty thousand francs? They talk of favouritism. It's only a step from that to assuming that Albert will get a percentage from the chosen family.

The BUTLER *comes in.*

BUTLER. Madame. I beg Madame la Duchesse's pardon. There are some more people demanding Maître Huspar or Madame la Duchesse.

DUCHESSE. Name?

BUTLER. They gave me this card, which I did not allow myself to present to Madame la Duchesse, as it is a tradesman's.

He reads, with great dignity.

Butter, eggs, cheeses. Maison Bougran.

DUCHESSE (*looking at her list*). Bougran? Did you say Bougran? It's the grocer!

The VALET *knocks and enters.*

VALET. I beg Madame's pardon, but there's a gentleman, or rather a man, saying he wants to see Madame la Duchesse. I must tell Madame that his appearance is such that I have not dared to bring him in.

DUCHESSE (*at her list*). Name? Legropâtre or Madensale?

VALET. Legropâtre, Madame la Duchesse.

DUCHESSE. It's the gasman! Bring him in. Show all deference. They've come by the same train, every one of them. I expect the Madensales will be here soon. I've telephoned Pont-au-Bronc. I'll try to keep them quiet.

She goes out quickly, followed by MAÎTRE HUSPAR.

GASTON (*harassed, murmuring*). You all have proofs, photographs, remembered crimes. I listen to you, each one of you, and I feel rising within me a mongrel being made up of a little of each of your sons, and nothing at all of me. Because your sons have nothing that is me. (*He repeats.*) Me! Me! I exist, in spite of your stories. You spoke just now of the wonderful simplicity of my life as a man with no memory. Now laugh! Try taking every virtue and every vice and slinging them round your neck.

VALENTINE (*who came in when the* DUCHESSE *went out*). It will all be much simpler if you'll listen to me just for a moment, Jacques. The inheritance I can offer may seem a little complicated, but at least it will free you from the others. Will you hear what I have to say?

55

GASTON. Yes.

VALENTINE. I'm supposed never to have seen you naked, isn't that right? Well, you have a very small scar about two centimetres long, under your left shoulder blade. I'm sure none of the doctors who've examined you will have seen it. Very small, it is. It was done with a hat pin. You know how we were rigged out in 1918. I gave it to you one day when I thought you'd been with another woman.

> *She goes out.* GASTON *remains, stunned for a moment. Then, slowly, he begins to take off his jacket.*

CURTAIN

SCENE FOUR

The CHAUFFEUR *and the* VALET *are climbing on a chair in a narrow dark passage to look through a small oval window.*

VALET. Look at that now! Look, out of his trousers . . .

CHAUFFEUR (*pushing him to take his place*). You're making it up, I'm sure. But look, he's struck, absolutely struck, that boy. Now, what's he doing now? Looking for what? A flea, must be looking for a . . . But wait, now, wait. He's climbing, yes, up on a chair to look at himself in the glass above the mantelpiece . . .

VALET. Now, you're making it up now. On a chair – climbing on a chair . . .

CHAUFFEUR. I said it. I said, on a chair . . .

VALET (*taking his place*). Let's see then. Ah, look at it! All that to look at his back! He's struck all right! Good,

56

he's getting down. He's seen what he wanted. Now he's putting on his shirt; now he's sitting down; now, now – God!

CHAUFFEUR. Now, what's he doing now?

VALET (*turning round, stupefied*). Crying . . .

CURTAIN

SCENE FIVE

JACQUES'S *bedroom. The venetian blinds are down, the reddish shadows streaked with light. It is morning.* GASTON *is in bed, asleep. The* BUTLER *and the* VALET *are in the act of carrying in the stuffed animals which they place around the bed. The* DUCHESSE *and* MADAME RENAUD *direct these goings on from the corridor. All play in whispers and on tiptoe.*

BUTLER. Shall we space them equally round the bed, Madame la Duchesse?

DUCHESSE. Yes, yes, round the bed, so that when he opens his eyes he'll see them all at the same time.

MME. RENAUD. If only these animals can bring back his memory!

DUCHESSE. They should make an impression.

MME. RENAUD. He loved hunting them so much. He'd climb the highest tree to put bird lime on the branches.

DUCHESSE (*to the* BUTLER). Put one of them very near to him. On his pillow. Yes, on his pillow.

BUTLER. Doesn't Madame la Duchesse feel that he may be frightened to wake and find an animal so near his face?

DUCHESSE. In his case, fright is an excellent thing. First class. (*She goes back to* MADAME RENAUD.) I won't hide

57

the fact from you, Madame, that I am consumed with worry. I managed to calm these people last night by telling them that Huspar and Albert would be here at daybreak this morning. But who can tell if we shall get out of this without . . .

The VALET *comes in.*

VALET. Monsieur Gaston's presumed families are here, Madame la Duchesse.

DUCHESSE. There you are! I said nine o'clock. They're here at five to. Nothing deters such people.

MME. RENAUD. Where have you put them, Victor?

VALET. In the drawing-room, Madame.

DUCHESSE. Is it the same crowd as yesterday? The working classes always come in large numbers, the better to defend themselves.

VALET. There are even more of them, Madame la Duchesse.

DUCHESSE. Even more! What does that mean?

VALET. Three more, but together. A gentleman of good appearance, with a little boy and his governess.

DUCHESS. What kind of governess?

VALET. English, Madame la Duchesse.

DUCHESSE. Ah! that will be the Madensales. Charming people, I believe. It's the English branch of the family which claims Gaston. Very touching, is it not, that they should come so far to recover one of their family? Ask them to be patient for a while, Victor.

MME. RENAUD. These people won't take him away before he has spoken, will they, Madame?

DUCHESSE. No, don't be afraid. You gave the first proof. Whether he likes it or not we must follow it to the end. Dear Albert has promised to be quite firm on that point. On the other hand, we must be very diplomatic if we're to avoid a scandal.

58

MME. RENAUD. I feel you exaggerate the danger of that, Madame.

DUCHESSE. Not a bit of it! The Left Wing press is lying in wait for Albert. Such people will leap on a calumny like dogs on carrion. I cannot allow that, even though I want Gaston to belong to a charming family. You are a mother; I am an aunt. Before all else. (*She clasps* MADAME RENAUD *by the arm.*) Understand, I am as heartbroken as you that so much of your proof carries sorrow and wretchedness with it.

The VALET *passes close to her with some stuffed squirrels. She follows him with her eyes.*

DUCHESSE. Squirrel skin is enchanting, isn't it? Why have I never thought of having a coat made of it?

MME. RENAUD (*taken aback*). I don't know.

VALET. It would be too small.

BUTLER (*who is watching at the door*). Monsieur is moving!

DUCHESSE. He mustn't see us. (*To the* BUTLER.) Open the shutters.

Full daylight in the room. GASTON *has opened his eyes. He sees something close to his face. He sits up in bed.*

GASTON. What —!

Around him he sees the stuffed weasels, polecats and squirrels. His eyes wide open, he shouts.

What are all these animals? What do they want?

The BUTLER *comes forward.*

BUTLER. They're stuffed, Monsieur. They're the animals Monsieur amused himself by killing. Doesn't Monsieur recognize them?

GASTON (*shouts in a harsh voice*). I have never killed animals!

He has got up from the bed. The VALET *rushes forward with his dressing gown. They go into the bathroom, but* GASTON *comes out at once, and returns to the animals.*

How did he catch them?

BUTLER. Surely Monsieur hasn't forgotten the steel traps he chose with such care from the catalogue of the Bicycle and Small Arms Works at Saint-Etienne. Of course, to make sure, Monsieur preferred bird lime.

GASTON. Then they were not dead when he found them?

BUTLER. Usually not. Monsieur would finish them off with a hunting knife. Very skilfully.

GASTON (*after a silence*). What can be done for dead animals?

He makes a shy gesture, not daring to let it become a caress. He stands for a moment in thought.

What do caresses mean to these stiff dry things? I'll give breadcrumbs and nuts to other squirrels every day. I shall allow no harm to come to the weasels on any land I may own. But how can I comfort these for their long night of pain and fear, held in relentless jaws, and not understanding why?

BUTLER. Oh, Monsieur needn't worry about that. It doesn't mean much to animals. And, besides, it's all over now.

GASTON (*repeats*). It's all over now. And even if I had the power to give happiness to every animal of the woods . . . True: it's all over now. (*He goes towards the bathroom, saying*) Why haven't I the same dressing gown as last night?

BUTLER. They're both Monsieur's. Madame told me to give

60

Monsieur all of them, in the hope that he would recognize one of them.

GASTON. What's in the pockets of this one? Reminders, like yesterday?

BUTLER (*following him*). No, Monsieur. Moth balls.

> *The bathroom door is shut again. The* DUCHESSE *and* MADAME RENAUD *come out of their hiding place.*

BUTLER (*with a sign to them before going out*). Madame will have heard what was said. I don't think Monsieur recognized anything.

MME. RENAUD (*crossly*). One would really think he's not trying.

DUCHESSE. Believe me, if that's so I'll speak very severely to him. But I'm afraid it's more serious than that.

GEORGES (*coming in*). Well, is he awake?

DUCHESSE. Yes, but our little trick has failed.

MME. RENAUD. He pretended to be surprised when he saw the animals, but that's all.

GEORGES. Would you leave me with him for a while? I'd like to try to say something to him.

MME. RENAUD. If only you can succeed, Georges! I'm beginning to lose hope.

GEORGES. You mustn't, Mamma. No, you must hope to the end. Even against the evidence itself.

MME. RENAUD (*a little irritably*). Really, his attitude is tiresome. I must say, he still seems very antagonistic towards me . . .

GEORGES. But he hasn't recognized you yet . . .

MME. RENAUD. Oh, he was always a bad lot! Even if he's lost his memory, why pretend he's changed?

DUCHESSE (*going out with her*). I think you exaggerate his animosity towards you, Madame. Far be it from me to give you advice, but I must say I find your way of going about it rather cold-blooded. You're a mother, damn it! Be moving, pathetic! Get on your knees! Weep!

MME. RENAUD. Madame, to have Jacques take his place here again is my dearest wish, but I really cannot go as far as you suggest. Especially after what has happened.

DUCHESSE. Pity. I'm sure it would touch him very much. Now, if someone tried to take darling Albert from me, I think I should become like a wild beast. D'you know, when he was refused his degree I pulled the beard of the dean of the faculty.

They go out. During this time GEORGES *has been knocking at the door of the room. Then, timidly, he goes in.*

GEORGES. May I have a word with you, Jacques?

GASTON (*from the bathroom, off*). Who is it now? I asked that no one should come in. Can't I even wash without being plagued by do I remember this, that and the other?

VALET (*through a crack in the bathroom door*). Monsieur is in his bath, Monsieur. (*To* GASTON, *who is unseen.*) It's Monsieur, Monsieur.

GASTON (*still irritable, but milder*). Oh, it's you, is it?

GEORGES (*to the* VALET). Leave us, Victor.

The VALET *goes out.* GEORGES *moves to the door.*

Forgive me, Jacques. I know how we've worried you with our stories. Even so, what I have to say is important. If it doesn't bore you too much, I hope you'll let me . . . (*He sits down.*)

GASTON (*from the bathroom*). What new beastliness have you raked up from your brother's past to shoulder me with?

GEORGES. No beastliness, Jacques. These are just thoughts. Thoughts I'd like to tell you about, if you'll let me.

He hesitates for a second, and then begins.

You know, pretending that one is an honest man, that one has never been anything else, and that one has never done wrong . . . That's quite easy for some people, after all . . . One believes that anything is justified. Such people speak to others from heights of serenity. They reproach, they complain. (*He asks abruptly.*) Didn't you feel that with me, yesterday?

The answer comes, irritably as before, reluctantly, a second later.

GASTON (*off*). What about?

GEORGES. In what I said to you. In my exaggerated pose as a victim. The sort of blackmailing I tried with my miserable story.

A noise is heard from the bathroom. GEORGES, *alarmed, gets up.*

No, don't come out here. Let me finish. I want it this way. If I'm with you face to face I shall put on a brotherly manner, and never lose it again. I did a lot of thinking last night, Jacques. What happened between you and Valentine was dreadful, certainly, but you were both children, weren't you? Then, when we were at Dinard before we were married, it was always with you that she wanted to go walking. Perhaps you were both in love, then: a couple of kids, you couldn't help it. I came between you, clumsy, older, with a position in life. I played the game properly, and her aunt had to force her to accept me. So, I came to a conclusion last night. It was this: I have no right to reproach you. I withdraw all I said. There!

63

He sits again in the chair. He can do no more. GASTON *has come out from the bathroom. He goes quietly to* GEORGES, *and puts a hand on his shoulder.*

GASTON. How could you love that little horror so much?

GEORGES. He was my brother.

GASTON. He didn't behave like a brother. He robbed you. He deceived you. You'd have hated your best friend if he'd done that.

GEORGES. A friend is not the same. He was my brother.

GASTON. And how can you want him back, even if he's older and changed, coming between you and your wife?

GEORGES (*simply*). Whatever you say, even if he was a murderer, he's one of the family. His place is in the family.

GASTON (*repeats, after a pause*). He's one of the family. His place is in the family. How easy that is! (*Speaking to himself.*) He believed himself to be good: he isn't. And honest: not very. He thought himself alone and, in spite of the asylum, free. But he has found the world full of people to whom he has given pledges, and who wait for him. So his smallest action can only be an extension of an old gesture. How easy that is!

Roughly, he takes GEORGES *by the arm.*

Why come and tell me this now? There's no point in it! Why sling your affection at me? Because that's even easier, I suppose. (*He sinks down on the bed, strangely tired.*) You have won.

GEORGES (*bewildered*). I don't understand, Jacques. Believe me, it wasn't easy to tell you that. But I spoke to comfort you. You must have felt very lonely since yesterday.

GASTON. Loneliness has not been my worst enemy.

GEORGES. I expect you've noticed the looks of the servants.

Or a feeling of constraint about the house. But you mustn't think that no one loves you. Mamma . . .

GASTON *looks up at him.* GEORGES *is made uneasy by this.*

But above all, Jacques, I loved you very much.

GASTON. Who else?

GEORGES. Well – (*he is embarrassed*) – if you will have it, Valentine, no doubt.

GASTON. We were lovers. It's not the same thing. There's only you.

GEORGES (*looking down*). Perhaps.

GASTON. Why should you? I don't begin to understand why!

GEORGES (*quietly*). Have you never dreamed of a friend? At the beginning, small boys together, walking hand in hand. Friendship delights you. Think then, how lucky you would be to have a friend so young that you could explore together the first attempt at your alphabet, take the first bicycle rides, and make the first try at swimming. So frail a friend that you must always protect him . . .

GASTON (*after a pause*). Was I quite small when your father died?

GEORGES. You were two.

GASTON. And how old were you?

GEORGES. Fourteen. I had to look after you. You were so very young. (*A pause. He gives his real reason.*) You've always been so young for everything. For the money we gave you, like fools: too much of it. For Mamma's hardness. For my weakness and clumsiness. You fought against the arrogance and violence in you when you were only two years old. They were horrors of which you were innocent, and from which we should have saved you.

Not only did we not know how to do that, we even accused you. We let you go alone to the war. Beneath your kitbag, rifle, gas mask and a couple of haversacks you were a very small soldier on the station platform.

GASTON (*shrugging his shoulders*). I expect the men with big moustaches and an impressive manner were also quite young. They, too, were being asked to do something beyond their power . . .

GEORGES (*cries out, almost in sorrow*). But you were only eighteen! And the first thing they asked you to do, having fed you on glory and heroism in a dead language, was to scrape out trenches with a kitchen knife.

GASTON (*with a laugh, which rings false*). And after that? To kill. It seems to me an excellent way of introducing a young man to life.

The BUTLER *comes in.*

BUTLER. Madame la Duchesse asks if Monsieur will be good enough to join her in the drawing-room when he is ready.

GEORGES (*getting up*). I'll go now. Despite everything that's been said, don't hate him too much. Jacques, I mean. I think really he was just – just a poor little boy.

He goes out. The BUTLER *stays with* GASTON, *helping him to dress.*

GASTON (*suddenly*). Tell me . . .

BUTLER. Monsieur?

GASTON. Have you ever killed someone?

BUTLER. Monsieur is fond of a joke. If I'd killed someone I'd not still be in Madame's service. Monsieur knows that.

GASTON. Not even during the war? Say, hand to hand, jumping into a dugout in the second wave of attack.

BUTLER. I spent the war as a corporal in the Quartermaster's Stores. The Army Service Corps had few opportunities to kill anyone.

GASTON (*motionless, quite pale, very quietly*). You're lucky. It's a frightening moment when you're on the point of killing someone in order to live.

BUTLER (*who does not know whether to laugh or not*). Monsieur is right. A frightening moment. Especially for the victim.

GASTON. You're wrong. It's all a matter of imagination, and the victim often has less imagination than the killer. (*A pause.*) Sometimes he is nothing more than a shadow in the murderer's dreams.

BUTLER. In that case, the victim would suffer little, to be sure.

GASTON. And the murderer, on his part, must suffer for both. Are you fond of life?

BUTLER. Yes, Monsieur, like everyone.

GASTON. Suppose that in order to live you had to strike into nothingness a young man. Eighteen years old. Arrogant, good for not much, but, all the same, just a poor little boy. You could be free, no one more so, but to be free you must leave an innocent corpse behind you. What would you do?

BUTLER. I couldn't allow myself to ask myself such a question, Monsieur. But, if I'm to believe what the detective stories say, you must never leave the body behind.

GASTON (*suddenly laughing*). Suppose no one – apart from the murderer – could see the body? (*He goes to the* BUTLER *and says, lightly*) Look, the thing is done. The corpse is at your feet. Can you see it?

The BUTLER *looks at his feet, jumps aside, looks around him and escapes, appalled, as fast as his dignity allows.*

67

VALENTINE *comes quickly along the corridor. She runs into the room.*

VALENTINE. I've been talking to Georges. Haven't you told them yet? I didn't want to be the first to come to your room this morning, because I thought they would call me with the good news. Why haven't you told them?

GASTON *stares at her without speaking.*

Well, at least don't keep me in suspense. The scar. You saw it yesterday. In the glass. I know you did.

GASTON (*quietly, still staring at her*). I didn't see any scar.

VALENTINE. What did you say?

GASTON. I looked very carefully at my back, and I could find no scar. You must have been mistaken.

VALENTINE (*she stares at him for a moment, stunned. Then understands and suddenly cries out*). I hate you! I hate you!

GASTON (*very calm*). It's better that way.

VALENTINE. Do you think that what you're about to do concerns no one but yourself ?

GASTON. Yes. I'm going to deny my past and the people in this house, including myself. Perhaps this is my family, you my mistress, all of it my proven history. But – I don't like you very much. I refuse to own you.

VALENTINE. You're mad! Criminal! You can't refuse your past, deny yourself.

GASTON. It's true that I'm probably the only man who has been given the chance of actually doing what everyone dreams about. I am a grown man, yet I can be as inexperienced as a child, if I wish. Not to make use of such a chance would be criminal. So I deny you. There are too many things I must try to forget since only yesterday.

VALENTINE. And my love for you. What are you going to

68

do about that? I suppose you're no longer interested.

GASTON. All I can see of your love at this moment is the hate in your eyes. No doubt that's an expression of love which would only surprise a man without a memory. Anyway, it's fitting, for it's what I wish to see. I am a lover who does not acknowledge love for his mistress, and who remembers nothing of the first kiss or the first tears. I'm not made prisoner by such memories, and, anyway, I'll forget everything tomorrow. To be able to do that is a fairly rare piece of luck, as well. I'm profiting by it.

VALENTINE. Suppose I tell everyone here that I recognize that scar?

GASTON. I've foreseen that happening. From love's point of view I'm sure that Valentine of the old days would have done that before now. It's comforting that you seem to have become more discreet. From the law's point of view you are my sister-in-law, and you claim to be my mistress. What court would dare to come to a serious decision on such a nasty little hole and corner affair, for which they have only your word?

VALENTINE (*pale, her teeth clenched*). Very well. Be high-handed. But, forgetting this business of your memory, don't think your behaviour is so out of the ordinary for a man. Underneath, I expect you're feeling rather pleased with yourself. Gratifying, isn't it, to refuse a woman who has waited so long! Well, forgive the pain this must cause you, but – I've had other lovers since the war.

GASTON (*smiling*). Thank you so much, but there was no pain.

The BUTLER *and the* VALET *appear in the corridor. From their byplay it can be seen that they thought it best to come together.*

69

VALET (*from the door*). Madame la Duchesse Dupont-Dufort begs Monsieur to hurry, and be good enough to join her at once in the drawing-room, because Monsieur's families are impatient.

GASTON *does not move. The servants go.*

VALENTINE (*with a sudden laugh*). Your families, Jacques! It's so silly it makes me laugh. Because that's something you've forgotten. If you refuse to come back to us you'll have to go to one of them, whether you like it or not. You'll have to sleep between the sheets of their dead man, put on his flannel vest and old slippers, which they will have devoutly preserved. Your families are impatient! Come along, then! You're so afraid of the past. Well, come and look at these lower-class families and see what kind of past, calculated and sordid, they have to offer you.

GASTON. It will be hard for them to do better than you in that way.

VALENTINE. Think so? The swindling and wasting of your half-million francs will seem nothing set beside their endless gossip of goings-on heard through the party wall, and the thick darned underclothes. Come along. As you don't want us, you must go to your other families now.

She pulls him by the arm. He resists.

GASTON. No, I'm not coming.
VALENTINE. Oh? Then what do you mean to do?
GASTON. I'm going away.
VALENTINE. Where?
GASTON. It doesn't matter where.
VALENTINE. Only a man without a memory talks like that. People with memories know that they must choose a

destination when they travel, and that they can only go as far as the price of the ticket allows. You must choose, Blois or Orleans. Certainly, if you had money the world would lie waiting before you. But you haven't a penny in your pocket. So what are you going to do?

GASTON. Upset your ideas. Walk. Across the fields, towards Châteaudun.

VALENTINE. Do you feel so free since you got rid of us? But, you know, to the police you'll only be an escaped lunatic.

GASTON. I shall be far away. I walk quickly.

VALENTINE (*she shouts in his face*). I shall give the alarm if you so much as take one step from this room!

GASTON, *suddenly, has gone to the window.*

Don't be a fool! The window's too high. That's no way out.

GASTON, *like a trapped animal, has come back to her. She looks at him, and then says quietly:*

You may get rid of us, but you'll never lose the habit of letting your thoughts show in your eyes. No, Jacques, no. Even if you kill me to get an hour without pursuit, you'll be caught.

GASTON, *his head lowered, has been driven into a corner of the room.*

For it's not only I who pursue and want to hold you. It's all men and all women, and even the dead who dimly feel that you are about to snatch yourself from them. You can't escape from the whole world, Jacques. Whether you want it or not, you must belong to someone. Or else go back to your asylum.

GASTON (*whispering*). Well, then, I'll go back to my asylum.

71

VALENTINE. You forget I once worked there for a day. I saw you planting lettuces, and happy, it's true; but I also saw you emptying and washing the pots, being bullied by the nurses, and begging them for a fill for your pipe. You're very arrogant with us. You speak curtly, and laugh at us. But without us you're nothing but a helpless little boy, who isn't allowed out alone, and who has to shut himself up in the lavatory to smoke.

GASTON (*at a sign to show that she has finished*). Go away, now. There's no longer any hope for me. You have done everything possible.

> VALENTINE *goes without a word.* GASTON *remains alone. Wearily, he looks round the room. He stands for a long time looking at himself in the wardrobe glass. Suddenly, he takes up something from the table near to him, and, without taking his eyes from his reflection, smashes it against the glass, which shatters to pieces. He sits on the bed, his head in his hands. Silence, then, softly, music starts: rather sad at first, then, little by little, despite* GASTON, *despite us, more lively. After a moment a* SMALL BOY, *in an Eton suit, opens the door of the ante-chamber and looks in, curiously. Then he carefully shuts the door and ventures into the corridor on tiptoe. He opens all the doors that he comes to on his way, and questioningly looks into each room. Coming to the door of the bedroom; he does the same. He finds himself confronted by* GASTON, *who looks up, surprised by this appearance.*

SMALL BOY. Oh, I beg your pardon, sir. Perhaps you could direct me. I'm looking for the little place.

GASTON (*coming out of his thoughts*). The little place? What little place?

SMALL BOY. The little place where you're left in peace.

GASTON (*understands. Looking at the* BOY *he suddenly, in spite of himself, bursts into real laughter*). If only it could be found! Believe it or not, I'm also looking for the place where you're left in peace . . .

SMALL BOY. I wonder who we could ask?

GASTON (*laughs again*). I wonder.

SMALL BOY. Anyway, you haven't much chance of finding it by just sitting there, have you? (*He sees the broken looking glass.*) Oh, I say! Did you do that?

GASTON. Yes.

SMALL BOY. I suppose it means you're very angry about something. Better to speak out, you know. After all, you're grown up. No one can do much to you. They say that brings bad luck.

GASTON. I know they do.

SMALL BOY (*going*). I'll look in the corridor to see if I can find a servant. If they tell me where it is I'll come back and let you know.

> GASTON *looks up at him.*

The place we're both looking for.

GASTON (*smiles*). Wait a minute. Your place, where you'll be left in peace, is much easier to find than mine. Yours is through there, in the bathroom.

SMALL BOY. Thank you very much, sir.

> *The* SMALL BOY *goes into the bathroom. The music again takes up its little mocking theme. After a few seconds the* SMALL BOY *comes back.* GASTON *has not moved.*

SMALL BOY. Now I must go back to the drawing-room. Is that the way?

GASTON. Yes. Are you with the families?

SMALL BOY. Yes, I am. The place is full of all kinds of

73

people who've come to try to recognize some man who lost his memory in the war. I'm here for that, too. We flew over at a moment's notice. Seems some dirty work is going on. I don't really understand what it's all about. You'd have to talk to Uncle Job. Have you ever been in an aeroplane?

GASTON. Which family do you belong to?

SMALL BOY. Madensale.

GASTON. Madensale. Ah, yes, the English people. I've seen the file. Degree of relationship: uncle. As a matter of fact, it was I who wrote out the label to stick on the file. So there must be an uncle in the Madensale family.

SMALL BOY. Yes, sir . . .

GASTON. Of course, Uncle Job, isn't it? Well, tell Uncle Job, will you, that if he takes my advice, he won't have too much hope on the subject of his nephew.

SMALL BOY. Why tell me that, sir?

GASTON. Because the chances are that the nephew in question won't recognize Uncle Job.

SMALL BOY. There's no reason why he should, sir. It's not Uncle Job who's looking for his nephew.

GASTON. Oh? Is there another Madensale uncle?

SMALL BOY. Yes, sir. It's really rather funny. I'm the Madensale uncle.

GASTON (*startled*). How can you be? You mean your father.

SMALL BOY. No, I mean me. It's rather embarrassing, as you can imagine, for a boy to be uncle to a grown up. It took me a long time to get used to it. My grandfather had children very late in life. That's how it happened. I was born twenty-six years after my nephew.

> GASTON *bursts into fresh laughter, and sits the* BOY *on his knee.*

GASTON. So you're the Madensale uncle.

74

SMALL BOY. That's right. But there's no need to laugh about it quite so much. I couldn't help it.

GASTON. But this Uncle Job you spoke about . . .

SMALL BOY. Oh, he's an old friend of my father's, the lawyer who looks after the business of my estate. I can't really call him Mister, so I call him Uncle Job.

GASTON. How does it come about that you should represent the Madensale family?

SMALL BOY. Because of a dreadful disaster. Have you ever heard of the wreck of the *Neptunia?*

GASTON. Yes. It was long ago.

SMALL BOY. Well, all my family went down on that cruise.

GASTON *stares at him in wonder.*

GASTON. All your relatives are dead?

SMALL BOY (*kindly*). Yes, but you needn't look at me like that. It's not so sad. I was still a very small baby when it happened. To tell the truth, I wasn't even aware of it.

GASTON (*puts the* BOY *down, looks at him, and then slaps him on the back*). Little Uncle Madensale, you're a very important person without knowing it!

SMALL BOY. I already play cricket very well. Do you play?

GASTON. But I don't understand why Uncle Job should come from the other end of England to look for your nephew, who, if anything, is going to complicate matters, I'd have thought.

SMALL BOY. That's because you don't understand the terms of the inheritance. It's very involved, but I think I'm right in saying that if we don't find my nephew a large part of the money will slip out of my hands. That would be a pity, because among the things I should inherit is a beautiful house in Sussex, with some fine ponies. Do you like riding?

75

GASTON (*thoughtfully*). So Uncle Job must be very anxious to find your nephew.

SMALL BOY. You can bet he is. For me and – well, also for himself. He's never said so, but my governess told me that he gets a percentage of the estate.

GASTON. I see. What sort of man is Uncle Job?

SMALL BOY (*innocently*). A rather plump gentleman, with white hair.

GASTON. No, I don't mean that. But, then, it's something you can't really tell me. Where is he at the moment?

SMALL BOY. In the garden, smoking his pipe. He didn't want to wait with the others in the drawing-room.

GASTON. Will you take me to him?

SMALL BOY. If you like.

GASTON (*rings. To the* VALET, *who comes in*). Tell Madame la Duchesse Dupont-Dufort that I have a very important message for her. Very important, you understand. Ask her to be so good as to come up.

VALET. A very important message. Right! Count on me, Monsieur. (*He goes out, excitedly, murmuring.*) Very important.

GASTON *takes the* SMALL BOY *to the opposite door.*

GASTON. Let's go this way.

Coming to the door he stops, and asks the BOY:

Are you quite sure that all your family are dead?

SMALL BOY. Every one of them. Even their closest friends, who were invited to make up the party on the cruise.

GASTON. Splendid!

He makes the SMALL BOY *pass before him, and they go out. The music starts again. The scene stays empty for a moment. Then the* DUCHESSE *comes in, followed by the* VALET.

DUCHESSE. Wants to see me, does he? Knows perfectly well I've been waiting for him. A message, did you say?

VALET. Yes. Very important.

DUCHESSE (*in the empty room*). Well, where is he?

> GASTON, *followed by* MR. PICWICK *and the* SMALL BOY, *comes into the room with great solemnity. Tremulo, or something of the sort, from the orchestra.*

GASTON. Madame la Duchesse, let me introduce Mr. Picwick. He is the solicitor for the Madensale family, of which this is the only representative. Mr. Picwick has told me something very disturbing. He says that his client's nephew had a faint scar, two centimetres long, under his left shoulder blade. Nobody knew about it. He learnt that it existed from a letter found by chance in a book.

PICWICK. I'll make the letter available to the asylum authorities on my return to England, Madame.

DUCHESSE. Have you never seen the scar, Gaston? Has no one ever seen it?

PICWICK. It's so small, Madame, that it could almost pass unnoticed.

GASTON (*taking off his shirt*). It's easy to prove. Will you look?

> *He pulls up his vest. The* DUCHESSE *raises her lorgnette.* PICWICK *puts on huge spectacles. In turning his back to them* GASTON *is facing the* SMALL BOY.

SMALL BOY. I hope it's there. I shall be very disappointed if you're not the man.

GASTON. Don't worry. I'm the man. Tell me, do you really remember nothing about your family? Not a face? Not even some detail?

77

SMALL BOY. Nothing at all. But if it worries you, I could try to find out.

GASTON. Don't bother.

DUCHESSE (*who has been looking at* GASTON'S *back, suddenly cries out*). There! There! Oh, my God! There it is!

PICWICK (*who has also been looking*). That's correct. Just there.

DUCHESSE. Kiss me, Gaston, kiss me. This is a miracle!

PICWICK (*without laughing*). And so unexpected . . .

DUCHESSE (*falls into a chair*). So frightening, almost. I think I'm going to faint.

GASTON (*helping her up, smiling*). I can't believe it.

DUCHESSE. Neither can I. I must telephone Pont-au-Bronc at once. Tell me, Monsieur Madensale, something I very much want to know. During the last blistering which Albert gave you he made you shout "Little Pisser" in your delirium. Is that a phrase which now takes its place in your former life?

GASTON. Ssh! Don't tell anyone. I was speaking to Albert.

DUCHESSE (*horrified*). Oh, the poor darling!

She hesitates a moment, then changes her mind.

It doesn't matter. I forgive you.

She turns to PICWICK, *simpering.*

Of course, I see now. It was just the English sense of fun.

PICWICK. That's right.

DUCHESSE (*suddenly thinking of it*). This will be a terrible blow to the Renauds. How can we tell them?

GASTON (*happily*). I leave it to you. I'm going out of this house in five minutes, without seeing them again.

DUCHESSE. Haven't you a message for them even?

GASTON. No. None. Well, yes . . . (*He hesitates.*) Yes. Tell

78

Georges Renaud that the fickle ghost of his brother surely sleeps safely in some common grave in Germany. He was just a child, deserving forgiveness for all things. A child Georges can now love without fear, for he need never see the ugly lines in the child's face as a man. There! And now . . .

He opens the door wide, showing them the way, charmingly. He holds the SMALL BOY *to him.*

Leave me alone with my family. We must compare memories . . .

The music is triumphant. The DUCHESSE *goes out with* PICWICK.

THE CURTAIN FALLS